*A Gift From:*

_____

*To:*

_____

# RANDOM ACTS OF Romance

Hallmark
BOOKS

RODALE

BOK 4028

This edition published in 2001 for Hallmark Cards, Inc., by Rodale Inc.

© 2001 by Rodale Inc.

Interior Photographs © by Comstock, p. 3; StockFood, p. 11; Corbis, pp. 17, 51, 90; Doug Menuez/PhotoDisc, p. 32; Nick Koudis/PhotoDisc, p. 36; EyeWire, p. 45; Anthony Saint James/PhotoDisc, p. 55; Jonnie Milles/PhotoDisc, p. 61; Mel Curtis/PhotoDisc, pp. 67, 109; Toupee/PhotoDisc, p. 72; Don Farrell/PhotoDisc, p. 79; Ryan McVay/PhotoDisc, p. 85; Buccina Studios/PhotoDisc, pp. 96, 135; Dgusa, p. 104; PhotoLink/PhotoDisc, p. 115; Alex L. Fradkin/PhotoDisc, p. 120; Wonderfile, p. 125; Jules Frazier/PhotoDisc, p. 131

Printed in the United States of America
Rodale Inc. makes every effort to use acid-free ♾, recycled paper ♻.

The following hopeless romantics contributed their talents and ideas to this book:
Molly Brown, Ken Winston Caine, Jack Croft, Sharon Faelten, Carol Gilmore, Kevin Ireland, Jennifer Kushnier, Eric Metcalf, Christian Millman, Wyatt Myers, Elly Phillips, Jacques Picard, Sally Reith, Elizabeth Shimer, Marie Suszynski, Mariska van Aalst, Julia VanTine

2   4   6   8   10   9   7   5   3      hardcover

# Contents

# Introduction

Have you ever watched a happy couple—still holding hands, still showing each other affection after years together—and wondered how they manage to stay so in love?

More than likely, the answer boils down to one word: romance.

Yes, romance is more than just the stuff of fairy tales, or a phase you pass through early in a relationship. It's a powerful tonic that can keep love burning hot forever—even when the routines of work, errands, friends, and kids threaten to put love on automatic pilot.

Within the pages of this book, you'll find more than 500 ideas for making romance a larger part of your love life. You'll discover unexpected or spur-of-the-moment ways to surprise your lover—what we call random acts of romance. You'll see simple gestures that you can use day after day to say "I love you." And, to inspire you, we've included dozens of real-life stories of clever and unusual ways that people have used romance to express their love. We hope you'll enjoy them all.

It doesn't take a lot to keep romance alive. Although extravagant gestures never hurt, you can spice up your life with just a warm touch, a quick kiss, an unexpected call, a thoughtful gift. The important thing is just to show your lover some attention, to confirm with your actions what you feel in your heart.

No, it doesn't take much. But ah, the results. . . .

# RANDOM
## ACTS FOR
*Everyday*
*Living*

# Simple Gestures
## that show you care

When you think romance, you may imagine moonlit beaches and expensive dinners, long-stemmed roses and horse-drawn carriages. But what really binds relationships is the routine: preparing dinner together, attending PTA meetings with your love, sharing chores like shoveling snow. Injecting romantic surprises into these commonplace moments can lift the weight of a challenging day, lace your hours with electricity and anticipation, and weave a few more threads into the tapestry of lifelong love.

A few seconds and a little imagination are all you need. Here are some suggestions to help you reconnect with your sweetheart during your ordinary times together each day.

In the midst of the morning rush, lean over, kiss your sweetheart's forehead, and say, "I'll miss you today."

♥

Look at your lover when she's not paying attention, then look away when she is.

♥

Go for a swing together in a hammock or a porch swing.

♥

Say "my love" so often that it becomes your partner's name.

♥

Get your wedding invitation or marriage certificate framed.

♥

Hire a cleaning service to spruce up the house, then take your lover for a romantic stroll while they clean.

♥

Find out your partner's birth flower and plant it in an inconspicuous spot. When it blooms, draw a map to the location and tape it to the bathroom mirror.

Tickle each other in an elevator.

♥

Treat your partner to a warm bath and pour in
essential oil of ylang-ylang or other musky
scents. When the bath is over, greet your love
with your fluffiest towel warmed in the dryer.

♥

Walk your love to the car in the morning. Open
the door, and after he's seated safely inside,
close it gently. Kiss the glass.

♥

Dress up for dinner.

♥

Show up at a parent-teacher conference when
you said you'd be too busy.

♥

## Extravagant
# G E S T U R E S

"When my boyfriend and I first started dating, he found out where my mother
and I were going for my birthday dinner. He bought 2 dozen red roses and
took them to the restaurant before we got there. During dinner, the waitress
brought them out with a card. It was so sweet—I couldn't wait for the dinner
to be over so I could find him and kiss him!"

Write your initials in a heart in the wet cement
of your sidewalk.

♥

Carry her over the threshold of your new
house—even if it's your third one!

♥

Give her a foot rub after a hard day.

♥

Call your mother-in-law "Dear."

♥

Buy the latest book by your sweetheart's
favorite author—on the day it's released.

♥

Meet her at the bus stop with a flower.

♥

Meet him at his car with an umbrella when it's
raining.

♥

Armed with a loofah, jump into the shower
with your lover, even when you're late for work.

♥

Learn a yoga pose that you can do together to
stretch out strained muscles.

# Extravagant GESTURES

*"My husband knew that the one thing I didn't like about our new home was its lack of trees. During the fall, before the first frost, he planted a whole stand of trees toward the back of our property. I never knew until they started to grow. Five years later, I look out of my kitchen window every day at the proof of his love."*

♥

Hold hands whenever you're together, whether you're at a cocktail party or just waiting in line at the grocery store.

♥

Brush your sweetheart's hair.

♥

Give your sweetie a scalp massage.

♥

Jump into a photo booth and kiss until all the pictures are taken.

♥

Whenever you hear "your song," grab your partner's hand and dance—no matter where you are.

♥

Put her pajamas in the dryer on a cold night.

# Extravagant
## G E S T U R E S

*My wife and I had been planning for months to redo the bathroom, but my work schedule just wasn't letting up. While I was on a business trip, she arranged for a contractor to report for duty 15 minutes after my plane took off. When I arrived home, she made me close my eyes and led me back into the bathroom—100 percent done and 100 percent beautiful.*

♥

Sneak a quick peck on the cheek when you think no one's looking; sneak another when they are.

♥

Come home earlier than you said you would and spend the extra time just hugging and talking to your love.

♥

Spend a day doing what your partner likes to do (shopping at the mall, attending a car show). Ask a lot of questions and try to learn why your lover enjoys it so much.

♥

Every day, spend 5 minutes listening, without interrupting, as your partner describes his day. Ask three questions about projects that you know your love is working on.

When you know that your sweetheart is in for a stressful week, iron all the shirts he'll need to get through the mornings easily.

♥

If she has to call in sick, do the same and tend to her sniffles.

♥

When you hear the bells of the ice cream truck, grab her hand and run outside.

## 15 Things I Wish My Partner Would Do

Sometimes you don't even have to be highly creative to show your romantic side. Here are 15 small ways that people on the street said their partners could demonstrate that they care.

1. Call my pot roast delicious even if it's really not.
2. Take the dog out in the morning without having to be asked.
3. Let me put my cold feet on him on a winter night.
4. Do the laundry for me.
5. Summon me by yelling, "Hey, Gorgeous."
6. Plan a Saturday with the kids and give me some alone time.
7. Remember my mother's birthday and suggest a gift.
8. Rub my feet while we watch TV.
9. Balance the checkbook for me.
10. Do the grocery shopping while I'm at work.
11. Kiss me on the neck when I least expect it.
12. Cook me a 16-ounce steak just the way I like it.
13. Hold the door open for me.
14. Tell me about the first time he realized he loved me.
15. Say, "I'm glad I get to grow old with you."

# *Extravagant* GESTURES

*My husband knew how much I loved to dance, but he was always too embarrassed to do it in public. The music would start, and I'd be squirming in my seat, or I'd dance with someone else. Unbeknownst to me, he started taking classes during his lunch hours. When my niece got married, the band played the first dance, and he got up and asked for my hand. I was so surprised, I nearly passed out. We danced the whole night away. He may not be Fred Astaire, but I was certainly floating on air!*

♥

Blow a kiss or send a wink from across a
crowded room.

♥

Give your lover a lottery ticket and a note
saying, "I hit the jackpot when I found you."

♥

# *Extravagant* GESTURES

*I once had a boyfriend who worked with me. He knew how much I loved fresh tomatoes from the garden. So he grew tomatoes, and every day he would bring me one. At lunch, he wouldn't even mention how special it was, just open his bag and get out this fresh tomato, cut it in half, hand me half, and smile.*

# Romance
## in the kitchen

When you consider all the comforts that flow from the kitchen, like warmth from the oven, delicious smells from baking food, and blissful contentment from a satisfying meal, it's not surprising that this special room holds the recipe for romance, too.

The ways that you can share special moments in the kitchen with your loved one are as endless as the combinations of ingredients that your cupboard can contain. But here are some ideas that you can cook up to sweeten the morning, spice up the evening, and refresh your love at any moment in between.

Each week, buy an exotic food or spice, and together prepare and enjoy a new dish containing it.

♥

Tuck love notes around the kitchen where your lover will eventually find them. Hide them in the flour canister, a box of cereal, or the silverware drawer.

♥

Ask your partner which food aromas bring back fond childhood memories. Prepare some of this food so he can smell it when he steps into the house.

♥

Place a love note or small gift in a watertight plastic bag and freeze it into a block of ice. Leave it in the freezer with a note that says, "You melt me."

♥

Bake goodies in the shape of a heart, such as pancakes made with pink food coloring, cookies, pizza with her favorite toppings—or even meat loaf!

♥

After your honey has gone to bed, set a small vase of flowers in the fridge so she'll see it first thing in the morning as she reaches for the juice.

On a chilly evening, heat your sweetie a cup of
cocoa and stir it with a cinnamon stick.

♥

Do the dishes together.

♥

Slow dance while you're waiting for your meal
to bake in the oven.

♥

Bake your favorite kind of bread with your love,
kneading the dough together.

♥

Hide a small gift in the back of a cupboard.

## The 11 Most Romantic Foods

Looking for some inspiration for a romantic meal? Here are foods
that some of the world's most romantic food lovers find especially
heartwarming.

1. Warm, gooey chocolate chip cookies
2. Strawberries
3. Lobster
4. Gourmet flavored cheeses
5. Éclairs
6. Grapes
7. Truffles
8. Champagne
9. Fondue
10. Shrimp cocktail
11. Sorbet

Make a cake and lick the bowl together.

♥

Hang a heart-shaped sun catcher on the
kitchen window with a note telling him how
much he lights up your life.

♥

Keep your kitchen stocked with romantic
breakfast ingredients, like berries, whipped
cream, pancake mixes, real butter, and tiny
sausages. When time permits, whip up a
spur-of-the-moment breakfast together.

♥

Enjoy a picnic in the snug comfort of your
kitchen: Lay out a quilt and some throw
pillows, then feast together on exotic cheeses,
fancy meats, and a bottle of wine.

♥

Toast marshmallows over the flames of your gas
stove, then use them to make s'mores with
graham crackers and chocolate bars.

♥

Feed each other grapes.

♥

Take a trip to the country during berry season
and pick baskets of plump berries to make
preserves that you can enjoy in the winter.

Prepare crab legs or lobster and do all the work
for your love. Crack the shells, pull out the
meat, dip it in melted butter, and feed it to your
partner with your fingers.

♥

Before digging into dinner each night,
take the time to express why you're thankful
for each other.

♥

The next time you order Chinese food, slip a
secret love message inside your sweetie's
fortune cookie.

♥

Grow fresh herbs on the kitchen windowsill.
Use them in fresh-baked bread or stir them
into a romantic massage oil.

♥

# *Extravagant* GESTURES

"When we first moved to this country, we didn't have much money at all. My

husband and I were very careful with every penny. But when he came home

with 16 red roses for me, all my concern flew out the window. He'd spent an

entire week's grocery money on them, but I couldn't have cared less. I tended

and cared for those roses so they lasted for weeks. They've lasted an eternity

in my mind."

Prepare a feast that will tempt all five
of her senses, like a chocolate-and-fruit tart.
Make the dessert, but hold a few ingredients
on the side. Then blindfold her and lead her
through the ingredients: Feed her a spoonful
of chocolate for taste; hold a cut lemon under
her nose for smell; guide her fingers to a
plump, fuzzy kiwi for touch; and break off
a piece of the crust for sound. When she's
done, take off her blindfold so she can
see the whole delicious dessert.

♥

Decorate the kitchen table with fresh-cut
flowers from the garden placed in a crystal vase.

♥

Write a note that wishes him a great day
and leave it on on the coffee maker
or inside the coffee can, so he'll see it first
thing in the morning.

# Romance
## on the road

When you're caught in traffic on the way to work, the kids are fighting in the backseat when you're doing errands, or you're just in the middle of a cross-country drive with your love, it's easy to overlook how romantic travel can be. But with a little imagination and a few small gestures, you can make fond memories whenever you hit the road.

Even when you're not traveling together, as in a morning commute, you can show the one you love that you care. Here are some simple things that you can do while out and about that will bring you and your sweetheart closer as the distance from home grows greater.

Leave a photo of you from a memorable
occasion on your honey's dashboard or tuck it
into the visor.

♥

Put a love letter on his windshield, with a
red-lipstick kiss to seal the envelope
and instructions not to open it until he
arrives at work.

♥

Call the disc jockey at your sweetheart's favorite
radio station and dedicate a song to her.

♥

Leave fresh-cut flowers on the driver's seat.

♥

Sneak to your lover's car at night and place an
aromatherapy diffuser on the floor so she's
greeted with her favorite scent when she gets in
the car to go to work.

♥

Put a note somewhere obvious in the car,
instructing your love to look in the glove box or
trunk, where a small present awaits.

♥

Put a big sign on the garage door that says,
I LOVE YOU MORE EVERY DAY. PLEASE HURRY
UPSTAIRS TO ME.

# *Extravagant* GESTURES

*One night over dinner, my wife and I were reminiscing with the kids about favorite times when we were younger. I mentioned that when I was in college, I used to have an old convertible, and I loved ending the day by driving into the sunset with the top down. When I got home the next night, there she was in the driveway, sitting in the passenger seat of a Corvette roadster she'd rented. She had already arranged for a babysitter, so we headed west—just cruising with the top down. We finally stopped at an overlook, watched the city lights turn on, and kissed like we were kids again. What an incredible night! What an incredible woman!*

♥

Record a tape with your song, lines of poetry, or funny stories from your time together. Put it in the cassette player in your love's car so that it plays when the car starts. End the tape with a message detailing your plans for a romantic date at the end of the day.

♥

When the two of you are on a trip, stop at a scenic overlook or secluded rest stop and explore your surroundings.

♥

At the airport, page your sweetie under a pet nickname.

Travel by train in a private sleeper car and pretend you're riding the Orient Express.

♥

Research, plan, and book a weekend or weeklong getaway without his knowledge, then surprise him with the trip itinerary or brochures all done up in a shirt box or tie box.

♥

When you're planning a long road trip together, buy her favorite novel on tape so she can relax and listen.

♥

Buy a world map, plot the course of your dream trip, then learn to say "I love you" in the languages of all the countries you'd visit.

♥

Put your hand on his as he shifts gears.

♥

Buy a comfortable car pillow and let your honey sleep while you're driving.

♥

Drive to where city lights don't shine, lay a blanket on the hood of your car or on the ground, and gaze at the galaxy, watching for shooting stars.

# Extravagant
## G E S T U R E S

"When I was a teenager, I had a little Volkswagen Bug. I also had a boyfriend named Peter. We both worked at a local restaurant. He was a few years older than me, and a year after I met him, he headed off to college. Well, on the day he was to leave, I happened to be working the 6:00 A.M. to noon shift. As I made my bleary way to my car at around 5:45 A.M., I saw that there were roses in my car. Not a bouquet of roses; oh, no. There must have been 2 dozen perfect roses, strewn beautifully across the reclined passenger seat. His parting gift to me—and so romantically extravagant. That man had style. And, of course, my heart."

♥

Rent a motor scooter for the two of you while on vacation and see the sights in the open breeze. Alternate drivers, and be sure to hang on tightly to your lover.

♥

During the holidays, drive around different neighborhoods to admire the festive lights. Switch drivers often so that you each can safely gawk.

♥

Spend your time together in the car reminiscing about your favorite times with each other.

Before switching drivers on a trip, adjust the seat and mirrors to meet your mate's needs.

♥

On a long trip, read to your partner while she drives.

♥

Rub your lover's neck while she's driving.

♥

Hang a necklace or a small memento tied to a string from the rearview mirror of your darling's car.

♥

Take a spur-of-the-moment trip without a destination, then stop at a cozy hotel for the night.

♥

Park your car in the woods, open the doors, turn up the music, and dance in the leaves.

♥

Test-drive a luxury car you could never afford and take turns being each other's chauffeur.

♥

Pack your bikes and drive to a quaint little town, a lush park, or a river towpath, then explore it on two wheels.

Surprise your mate by stopping at a roadside attraction that you know she'll appreciate, such as a garage sale, a fruit stand, or a horse farm.

♥

Pretend you're newlyweds by making a JUST MARRIED sign for the back of your car, then drive around town beeping your horn and smiling. If your budget allows, book the bridal suite at a local hotel.

♥

Tell your love that you're having tire trouble and pull off the road in a scenic setting. Then, instead of the spare tire, pull a blanket and picnic basket out of the trunk and have a surprise picnic.

♥

## Extravagant GESTURES

*While traveling through Virginia with my husband, I saw a 1966 candy-apple red Mustang convertible for sale. I had a car just like that when I was 20, and I loved it! I told my husband I'd always wished I could have that car back, but I assumed nothing would come of my fantasy. However, while he was on a business trip the next week, he arranged to buy that car and then gave it to me as a 20th anniversary present. And, as if that weren't enough, he had 20 red roses delivered to the restaurant where we celebrated our anniversary.*

Take a ride in the vibrant fall foliage. Stop and collect leaves.

♥

Borrow your partner's car during the day and return it vacuumed, washed, and waxed.

♥

Take a sunrise paddle in a canoe and watch the sun burn the mist off the lake.

♥

Take a carriage ride and drink wine or hot cider, depending on the season.

♥

Go through a car wash, and while the brushes are soaping your windows, kiss like teenagers.

♥

Instead of watching television at night, take a spur-of-the-moment moonlit drive along a shore, through woods, or over rolling hills.

♥

Stop at a roadside souvenir shop and get a penny stamped with I LOVE YOU, your names, and the date.

# Romance
## in the bedroom

We spend a third of our lives in the bedroom, so it's understandable when we let a bit of the real world seep in— a pile of laundry over here, a to-do list over there. It's understandable, yes, but that doesn't mean that you should let this special place become just another outpost of your busy life.

The bedroom is the heart of your home, the space in which you and your partner are most a couple. If you want to make it Romance Central, you need to fill those four walls with things that make you feel good. Reserve it for peace, love, and rest; feed it clean sheets, fresh air, and warm and willing bodies; then spice up your time there with a few of these hints.

# Extravagant
## GESTURES

*My boyfriend had promised me a massage, and he set up the bedroom with candles and massage oil. He had me lie down and close my eyes. Then he poured a whole bagful of daisies—my favorite flower—all over me and the bed. The best part was thinking of him picking all those daisies for me!*

♥

Quietly turn off your partner's alarm clock before it rings. Prepare his clothes, keys, and work items. Let him sleep the extra minutes, then wake him up with a kiss on the cheek.

♥

Buy glow-in-the-dark stars and place them in constellations around the room. After you turn off the lights, hold each other until they fade out.

♥

Splurge on one set of 250-thread-count, all-cotton sheets. Wash them five times with lavender-scented water to get them nicely worn in and smelling lovely.

♥

Establish a nightly ritual: Hold hands, go outside to bid the moon good night, lock the doors, and kiss on the threshold of your bedroom.

Catch fireflies and watch them fly in
the pitch blackness from the comfort
of your cozy bed.

♥

Buy several yards of thin cotton muslin and
string up a makeshift canopy from hooks in the
ceiling.

♥

Before you go to sleep, "spoon" together and
wish each other sweet dreams.

♥

Read *1,001 Arabian Nights* to each other,
taking turns each night.

## Spice Up Your Bedroom

While potpourri may add a nice fragrance to your sweaters, the true
scent of romance is spice. Here are three can't-miss ways to work
spice into your life.

♡ Mix nutmeg, cinnamon, and cloves and heat them in a cup of
water on your stove or in the microwave oven. Then bring the
simmering brew into your bedroom and let its fragrance envelop
you and your lover.

♡ Mix some cinnamon oil with safflower oil to dilute it (essential oils
can burn your skin if you use them full strength). Then touch your
wrists and the pulse point at your throat with the mixture. The heat
from your body will carry the scent around the room.

♡ Sandalwood has long been linked with passion. Wash with
sandalwood soap before you head to bed, or burn a stick
of sandalwood incense.

Talk to your partner while he's sleeping; touch his cheek, and tell him you love him.

♥

If you wake up without any covers, don't tug them away from your lover. Instead, gently tuck them around her and get another blanket from the closet.

♥

Put a heating pad under the blankets for 20 minutes before you go to bed, then share the warm spot together.

## Make Your Bedroom into a Boudoir

Once you've selected the perfect sheets, stocked up on candles, and added a bit of spice to the air, try these extra hints to turn your bedroom into a romantic boudoir.

♡ Screen off any visual unpleasantries with a wicker, lacquer, or Victorian cloth screen, draped suggestively with scarves or other flowing fabric.

♡ Hang layered, translucent cotton curtains that let sunlight in but shield you from prying eyes. They'll give your room an exotic appeal.

♡ Place a thin silk scarf over each lamp to diffuse the light.

♡ Cold floors can chill a hot moment; if you don't have carpeting (or if your carpet could use a boudoir boost), add plush rugs or oriental carpets.

♡ Strategically place mirrors so that they catch candlelight and add to your room's ambience.

♡ Pile up pillows and cushions in seductive mounds around the room—you never know where your fancy will strike!

String your biggest floor plant with small white lights.

♥

Catch some butterflies, then release them into the bedroom to wake your lover on a sunny Sunday.

♥

Buy a massage oil formulated from her favorite scents—lemon, mint, lavender, or whatever—and use it often.

♥

Get a CD player for the bedroom and hide it behind a plant. Put on Ravel's *Bolero* and select "continuous play."

♥

Make the bed with satin sheets and have fun pulling each other around; wear satin pajamas for even more slide!

♥

Always have a full supply of candles and wooden matches around. Light the candles nightly.

♥

The next time it rains, put a baking sheet outside the window and listen to the patter as you fall asleep.

Share a bowl of strawberry ice cream in bed.

♥

Turn off the evening news. Turn on the
Romance Channel.

♥

Before you turn out the lights, look into each
other's eyes and tell each other why you're
thankful you had another day together.

♥

Tuck your partner in. Smooth her hair
and kiss her forehead before getting into bed
yourself.

## The Most Romantic Songs

When you're looking for a night of romance, here are some songs
that are guaranteed to spark the mood.

♡ "Just the Way You Are"
♡ "St. Elmo's Fire"
♡ "As Time Goes By"
♡ "Nights in White Satin"
♡ "Stardust Memories"
♡ "Wonderful World"
♡ "When a Man Loves a
Woman"
♡ "Three Times a Lady"
♡ "Shining Star"
♡ "Don't Know Much"

♡ "Just the Two of Us"
♡ "Always on My Mind"
♡ "You Are So Beautiful"
♡ "Wind beneath My Wings"
♡ "First Time Ever I Saw Your
Face"
♡ "Up Where We Belong"
♡ "Sometimes When We
Touch"
♡ "(Everything I Do) I Do It for
You"

Spend an evening in romantic silence—no
words allowed, just body language.

♥

Write with your finger on your mate's back and
have her guess what you're writing.

♥

Hang mistletoe over the middle of your bed—
year-round.

♥

Put a prism in the window so the morning light
will wake you with the sun's full spectrum.

♥

Find a few of her childhood stuffed animals
and set them around the bed.

♥

Set up a tent in your bedroom for an indoor
camp-out. Pretend to be a friendly bear.

♥

Install a small bubbling fountain to create
romantic sounds.

# Romance
## at the movies

For more than a century, movie lovers have been stealing away to theaters to enjoy an hour or two of action, suspense, and, of course, a little romance on the screen and off.

How could a setting like this not warm your emotions a few degrees? Soft seats in the cool darkness, your honey next to you, and silver-screen lovers weathering life's dramas to ride off into the sunset hand in hand.

Of course, there always are opportunities to spice things up a bit. The next time you head out to the movies or rent a video to watch at home, try a few of these ideas. When the film is over, the romance will just be heating up.

Arrange with the usher to bring her a surprise,
like a gift or a flower, just before the lights go
down.

♥

Sit in the back, where you can cuddle in the
darkness without anyone seeing you.

♥

Kiss each time the characters on screen kiss.

♥

Take turns picking the type of movie you see.
For every action movie, choose a romantic one,
and vice versa.

♥

Slip a line of dialogue or other reference to a
favorite movie into a casual conversation, so only
the two of you know what you're referring to.

♥

Use a pocketful of trivia cards from a romance
game to quiz each other until the movie starts.

♥

Never complain about a film that your loved
one has chosen.

♥

Whenever you both especially enjoy a film, buy
the soundtrack to listen to later.

After the movie, sit all the way through the credits and share one kiss for each person in the crew who worked as a "grip."

♥

Rent the video of the first movie you saw together, turn out the lights, and enjoy this early date all over again. Afterward, talk about how your lives have changed since you first saw the movie.

## The Most Romantic Movie Scenes

Have you ever seen a movie scene so hot that you wished you could jump right into the screen and turn into one of the characters? Here are a few that really get the sparks flying.

**Last of the Mohicans:** In desperate danger, Daniel Day-Lewis gives Madeleine Stowe a passionate kiss, then begs her to stay alive, reassuring her that he'll find her no matter what happens.

**Say Anything:** John Cusack wins Ione Skye's heart with a boom box held high over his head, pumping out a romantic song.

**Titanic:** Leonardo DiCaprio takes Kate Winslet out of her upper-crust world and down to the lower deck of the ship for some raucous dancing.

**Shakespeare in Love:** Joseph Fiennes and Gwyneth Paltrow lounge in bed reading *Romeo and Juliet* to each other.

**The Fabulous Baker Boys:** Michelle Pfeiffer stretches out across the piano as she sings "Makin' Whoopee" to pianist Jeff Bridges.

**Out of Africa:** Robert Redford gently washes Meryl Streep's hair against an exotic African backdrop.

**An Officer and a Gentleman:** Richard Gere strides into the factory in full-dress uniform to claim his beloved, Debra Winger.

**Body Heat:** William Hurt passionately breaks down the patio door in his haste to get to Kathleen Turner.

**Jerry Maguire:** Tom Cruise finds just the right words to say to Renee Zellweger: "You complete me."

Go to two movies in a row and take advantage
of a double dose of darkness.

♥

Ask the theater to run a special message on the
screen before the show starts.

♥

Rent a movie with a sensual food scene and
prepare a snack that's included in the film (for
example, *Like Water for Chocolate* or *Tom Jones*).

♥

Put your hand on her knee.

♥

Reach for his hand, even if the movie's not scary.

♥

Hold hands while you're in line to buy tickets.

♥

Rent the movie theater and stage a private
screening.

♥

Hide a small wrapped gift in his popcorn.

♥

When you get home, act out a romantic scene
from the movie.

# Romance
## at work

Let's admit it: It's not always easy to be romantic when you're at work and your mind is occupied with thoughts of the next sale, a project that needs to be finished by Friday, or that critical presentation you have to make in 2 weeks. But really there's no better time to be thinking of your sweetheart. It not only puts you in a better mood, it surely brightens your partner's day, too. (And just imagine how jealous your lover's officemates will be when that special something from you arrives.)

To show your lover that you really care, try these simple heart pleasers. They're guaranteed to spark a little romance.

Leave a business envelope in his briefcase with a note inside that describes why you fell in love with him.

♥

Drive your honey to work—right to the front door—and don't let her out of the car until you give her a big hug, look into her eyes, and say, "I couldn't live without you."

♥

If you see your mate leaving for work with an armload of items, offer to either go along or follow in your car, so that you can help carry some of the things.

♥

Serve her dinner and coffee when she has to bring work home, and ask what you can do around the house that would help her get her work done.

♥

Start a romantic short story about lovers similar to you who live in some exotic place, then send it via e-mail. Ask your lover to add a paragraph and send it back. Add something new to the story each week.

♥

Before work, go out for breakfast with your love and order something fancy: crepes or French toast, eggs Benedict, and a cappuccino or latte.

# Real-Life ROMANCE

*After a particularly grueling day at work, I walked into the parking lot. From a distance, I thought I saw someone behind the wheel of my car, and I got a little nervous. As I inched closer, I had to laugh. Knowing that I love the cartoon character, my boyfriend had bought a 3-foot-tall Curious George and put him behind the wheel, where he sat as if waiting to drive me home.*

♥

Place a sign that says I MISS YOU outside your mate's office window.

♥

Write a sweet note and put it in your honey's date book on the page for a month from now.

♥

On your partner's birthday, have a 6-foot hoagie delivered to his workplace so all his coworkers can partake, too.

♥

Pick him up at work wearing your best dress and take him to dinner—for no special reason.

♥

Meet for a quiet lunch in a park or arrange to have a picnic catered and hire a violinist to serenade you.

Send your sweetheart a brief e-mail at work that says something like, "Did I ever tell you that your eyes are beautiful and drive me absolutely crazy?" Update the message each week with praise for something else you really like about your love.

♥

Drop off an elegantly wrapped present at the office when your sweetheart is out to lunch.

♥

On her birthday, bake cookies or brownies, then hand-deliver one to each of her coworkers; she'll be the envy of them all.

♥

Hire a massage therapist to visit your lover at the office for a relaxing neck and shoulder massage.

♥

# Extravagant
## G E S T U R E S

My girlfriend knew I was having a tough time at work—every morning I dreaded my drive to the office. One morning, she got up early and stapled red cardboard hearts to trees along my entire route. At first I didn't realize it was for me, but because I take so many shortcuts, I figured it out pretty quickly. By the time I got to work, I was so touched, I didn't even think about the day ahead!

# Real-Life ROMANCE

*After a long day at work, my boyfriend took me to a local park halfway up the Rockies to listen to live chamber music. By the first intermission we realized we were both hungry, since neither of us had stopped to eat during the day. So we walked over to a beautiful restaurant in the middle of the park to eat dinner. We sat outside on a huge wraparound porch that looked out over the mountains. We talked and ate until a half-moon came out and illuminated the top of the mountain range. Then we walked out into the middle of an open field, spread out the blanket, and watched shooting stars while eating petit fours. We shared a kiss, and I felt like a teenager. We didn't leave until the sprinkler system chased us out of the park. It was a perfect night.*

♥

Create a cute code name to give the secretary or receptionist when you call so your lover will know it's you.

♥

Set up your sweetheart's computer screen to show a honeymoon photo or other special scene.

♥

Pick him up at work on a Friday with his luggage packed. Blindfold him after he gets in the car, then drive to a bed-and-breakfast for a weekend of romance.

Slip a revealing photo of yourself into your
mate's lunch bag.

♥

Pick up your sweetheart at lunch and go
shopping for a "just because" gift.

♥

Put a memento of your lover in your office and
replace it with a new one each week.

♥

Call the boss and arrange to "kidnap" your
honey from work for a few hours.

♥

Find a poem by her favorite poet—or,
better yet, write your own—and recite it
on her voice mail.

♥

## Extravagant
### G E S T U R E S

One month after we were married, on Valentine's Day, my husband (a military officer) hand-delivered 2 dozen red roses to my office. He waited while I read his "little" love note in front of all my very envious coworkers. It reminded me of the scene from An Officer and a Gentleman. It took all I had to keep from bursting into tears.

# Real-Life ROMANCE

*My honey called my office voice mail in the middle of the night, saying that if she had one wish, it would be to lie in my arms, even for just a moment. Wow!*

♥

When she comes home from a hard day at work, wash her hair.

♥

On a warm, sunny day, arrange a picnic outside your honey's office, complete with blanket, umbrella, and gourmet lunch foods, so the two of you can lounge in front of everyone who's madly working through lunch.

♥

If your partner works outside, page him and enter the numbers 07734 so that he can turn his pager upside down and read "hello." Or create another code number between the two of you that will let him know that you were thinking of him.

# THE
## LANGUAGE
## of Love

# Romantic
## writing

It's no accident that writing is the primary language of love. It's often easier to express your love in writing than in person. But even if what you're saying is entirely scripted, you can still surprise your sweetheart with the way you deliver it. Ambush your mate with a note placed where he will least expect it. Deliver an "I love you" from afar. Slip a special poem into your sweetheart's briefcase or lunch bag. There's no shortage of ways to surprise your lover and show your amorous side. With a little ingenuity and ideas like these, you can make every day Valentine's Day.

Tuck a love note inside the towel or sneakers your partner takes to the gym.

♥

Next time you're at the beach, take a photo of your names written in the sand and leave it behind the sun visor in your partner's car.

♥

Write your own poem (with the help of the rhyming tool on www.rhyme.lycos.com, if you need it). Then hang your poem on the handle of the refrigerator or tape it to your lover's favorite drink inside the refrigerator.

♥

## *Real-Life* ROMANCE

"One year for my birthday, when my husband and I were saving money to buy a house, I told him I didn't want him to spend anything on a present. So he used his imagination! With some of the kids' crayons, markers, and construction paper, he made me a card, which included a "gift certificate" for a night out for the two of us at a restaurant and movie of my choice. He drew pictures and wrote sweet little things that he loves about me. I still have it—about 3 years later. I was so touched that he would take the time and thought to make it that I told everyone I knew about it. It's the most romantic thing anyone has ever done for me, and the most memorable present I've ever received."

# Extravagant
## G E S T U R E S

*My wife hid hundreds of little pieces of paper that said "I love you" in everything I own. That was 3 years ago, and I still find them in shoes, drawers, etc.*

♥

Sit down with your sweetheart at a candlelit table and write "anniversary vows" so you can express how much you love and care for each other. Recite them every year.

♥

Slip a note into the adventure or romance novel that your partner is reading, saying, "This story is exciting, but we have it beat by a mile."

♥

Embroider your mate's socks or underwear with *your* initials.

## She Cheered Me Up with a Card

"I was having trouble with my stepmother and father and really felt unloved and unappreciated by them. I didn't really think that my wife understood the extent of my pain, until she walked through the door and handed me a card that said, 'I know that you're hurting right now, and I don't really know how to fix it. But I want you to know that you're never alone or unloved or unappreciated as long as I'm alive.' Boy, did I need that card right then. I smile every time I recall how lucky I truly am."

When you're on vacation together, address to your honey a postcard that says, "Having a wonderful time with you! Let's do this again." Mail it home.

♥

Buy balloons in your partner's favorite color. Fill each with air and a card that gives a reason that you love her. Scatter them around the room and join the fun in helping her pop them.

♥

Once a month, buy your honey a small gift that starts with a different letter of the alphabet: A for almonds, B for back-scratcher, C for corkscrew, and so on.

♥

Secretly bury a "love capsule" in your backyard. Include a small bottle of spirits and drink glasses, or another surprise, along with a love letter on parchment paper. Later that day, send your love on a hunt to find the treasures.

♥

## Real-Life ROMANCE

*After a couple of dates with a guy, I decided it wasn't working out, so I ended things. Then in a book he'd lent me I found a note from him, pouring his heart out about his feelings for me. I called him pronto.*

If you have a dog or cat that is up to the task, have him deliver a love note to your sweetie. Attach the letter to his collar and send him into the appropriate room.

♥

Make a personal invitation to a private tickling session, specifying the date, time, and location. Include a feather in the envelope and have one on hand for yourself when the action begins.

♥

Make your own personalized stationery on a computer or even a copy machine. Include snapshots of the two of you or draw humorous stick-figure images.

♥

Create your own romantic message in a bottle. Make an attention-getting label and put it someplace unusual, like inside a toolbox or sewing kit.

♥

Write a short script on how easy your partner is to love. Secretly record it as a home video. Include interviews with family and friends. Invite him to a private showing.

♥

Write a romantic message and attach it to the inside of the shower curtain so your honey can see it when he steps into the tub.

*For Christmas, instead of giving her an expensive piece of jewelry, I gave my girlfriend a telescope. The card attached to it said, "You showed me a new world. I can only repay you by showing you the universe."*

♥

Create a secret "I love you" signal—a clasped hand, a raised eyebrow, a half-smile—and use it often when you're in public, especially when you're each talking to different people.

♥

Freeze a small, folded note in an ice cube and place it in her drink or in a punch bowl.

♥

Find an old love note or e-mail from early in the relationship and slip it into your honey's pocket.

♥

Steam open a bill, insert a romantic note, then reseal the envelope and wait for your sweetheart to find it.

♥

With a toothpick, carve "[your initials] loves [your partner's initials]" in a fresh tub of margarine and wait for your lover to discover it.

# Love talk

*True love talk enlists the mind, body, and spirit to communicate affection, honesty, gentleness, sincerity, intimacy, caring, kindness, respect, and the joy you feel simply knowing that you love and are loved by a special person.*

*That's a lot to say, but there are so many ways to express it. You can make your point with one word and a special glance. You can say how much you appreciate your honey and offer a tender touch when your sweetheart least expects it. You can put your feelings in a song. The important thing is to make your words resonate. Here are some specific suggestions for speaking your words of love.*

Make a list of 10 things you admire most about your partner. Then call your lover at the same time each day for 10 days. Say, "I just called to tell you that . . ." and recite one of the items from the list.

♥

Let your partner know that even now, after all these years, sometimes when you talk to her on the phone or catch a glimpse of her in the distance, you feel a tingly rush of longing and desire and giddiness.

♥

If you're working late, call your spouse when you know that he or she is relaxing or ready for bed, and recount how you first met and all the wonderful feelings and thoughts and experiences you've shared.

♥

## *Real-Life* ROMANCE

One day when my husband was visiting with his family in our hometown, I took our kids to see how the organist played the old-fashioned church bells. As we walked up to the church, I heard a song that I recognized, but couldn't place, coming out of the tower. Suddenly I realized it was "Red Roses for a Blue Lady"—our song. My husband had arranged for the organist to play the song at the exact time we were to walk up the street.

Stay up all night talking and teasing.

♥

When you're out dancing, slip the bandleader
$5 and request that the next love song be
dedicated from you to your partner.

♥

Compliment your partner on some small thing
he does well, whether it's simply being a careful
driver, or cooking a wonderful meal, or being a
loving, steady part of your life.

♥

Find a romantic novel with very short chapters,
then call and read one chapter at a time each
day when you know your sweetheart will have
time to listen. Don't converse first—just read.

## Top 10 Songs with "Love" in the Title

1. "I Will Always Love You"
2. "Because You Loved Me"
3. "I Want to Be Loved By You"
4. "(Your Love Has Lifted Me) Higher and Higher"
5. "Crazy Love"
6. "Can't Help Falling in Love"
7. "It Must Be Love"
8. "(Are You Ready for) A Thing Called Love"
9. "Love Me Like a Man"
10. "Endless Love"

# Extravagant GESTURES

*I hate going to those hardware superstores, but my boyfriend managed to get me to go with him on an errand on my birthday. When we got to the lumber department, I found out that he had convinced the management to play "This Guy's in Love with You" over the intercom. Then he struck into the worst lip sync and pulled a gift out of his pocket. We got out of the store and started a very romantic evening.*

♥

Tell other people the special things you admire
about your lover—both in and out of your
partner's presence.

♥

Whisper "I love you" into your honey's ear while
slow dancing in public, or while dining, or
while standing in the theater line.

♥

Smile when you call your partner on the phone.
And keep smiling while you talk.

♥

After your lover has dealt with a difficult
situation, say, "I'm proud of the way you
handled that."

# The Language
## of flowers

Perhaps more than anything else, flowers are deeply
intertwined with romance. You can send flowers to celebrate
joyful moments, to lift your lover's spirits, to remind that
special someone of the way you feel. And yes, flowers also
help to say that you're sorry when things didn't quite go the
way you'd planned. Flowers are in every part of a romantic
relationship. Indeed, they symbolize the romantic life
itself: beautiful, enduring, colorful, yet fragile. And like
romance, flowers cannot be ignored or they wither. Here
are some passionate ways to use these eternal symbols to
express your love.

Ask a florist to save discarded rose petals for you. Sprinkle them in the bath, on the bed, over the tablecloth, or anywhere else.

♥

Sprinkle some edible violets over your partner's breakfast cereal.

♥

Find a daisy. Pull all the petals off and leave it with a note that reads, "It says you love me."

♥

Place one rose after another in a trail leading from the front door to a romantic dinner in the dining room.

♥

Press a wildflower in the book your lover is reading.

## The Meaning of Roses

All roses signify something special when you give them to the people closest to you. But certain colors have developed certain meanings over the years. Here are the most common.

♡ Red: Love, eternal love, respect, or courage
♡ Yellow: Friendship, joy, gladness, or freedom
♡ Pink and peach: Gratitude, appreciation, or admiration
♡ White: Innocence, purity, or reverence
♡ Red and white together: Unity

Scatter some wildflower seed along a stretch of road that your partner takes to work. When it blooms, it'll be a reminder of your love every time she passes by.

♥

Give her a gift certificate for 12 bouquets of mixed flowers over the next year.

♥

Come up with a list of 20 types of flowers. In a note, compare your beloved to each one. "You are sweeter than a lilac. . . . You are more sensuous than a rose. . . ."

♥

In the winter, pack some clean snow in a vase. Place a bouquet of flowers in the middle with a note that reads, "You make me bloom in winter."

♥

Take your love a different flower every day for a month. Or make it different colors of roses for a week.

♥

Pick a half-dozen different flowers. Hold each one under your partner's nose and have him guess what kind it is. If he's right, he wins a kiss.

Get some glue, some paper, and a large handful
of different wildflowers. Pluck the petals,
remove the leaves, trim the stems, and glue
everything into a mosaic or other picture for
your lover.

♥

With your partner, plant various types of
flowers at the same time. Make the one that
blooms first your own special flower.

## Monthly Flowers

You probably already know that each month has its own birthstone.
But did you know that every month also has its own birth flower?
Give your sweetheart a bouquet of her month's flower on her next
birthday.

**January:** White carnation, which signifies pure and deep love, good
luck

**February:** Violet, which means modesty, virtue, faithfulness

**March:** Daffodil, which means "love me," affection returned, desire,
sympathy

**April:** Sweet pea, which means "goodbye," departure, bliss,
"thank you"

**May:** Lily of the valley, meaning sweetness, humility

**June:** Rose, which means love, respect, beauty, youth

**July:** Delphinium, which signifies ardent attachment

**August:** Gladiolus, meaning sincerity

**September:** Aster, signifying love, daintiness

**October:** Marigold, which means sacred affection

**November:** Chrysanthemum, meaning optimism, cheerfulness

**December:** Narcissus, meaning formality

# Extravagant
## G E S T U R E S

*I met a man while I was out dancing one night. I told him how I loved the different colors and scents of different roses. Since he was in town for only one night, I didn't think the comment would be significant. Three weeks later I received a call at work. He had traced my name through my ex-husband! He was calling from 500 miles away to ask me for a dinner date that night.*

*He came to town, got pizza for my boys, and we went out. He'd taken the time to visit the restaurant before our date and had set a yellow rose at my place. After dinner he excused himself to go to the restroom, and while he was away he put a pink rose on my windshield. We went dancing, and he arranged for a different rose to be brought every hour. White . . . fire and ice . . . sterling . . . miniature. Then he excused himself once again. This time he went to my car and placed a red rose on the front seat. Needless to say, the rainbow of rose petals was incredible.*

♥

Place some bee stickers on a large photo of
your partner. Write along the side, "They
mistook you for a rose."

♥

Draw a picture of a beautiful flower. Write
underneath, "I tried to draw a picture of you,
and this is what came out."

Leave flowers sticking out of your sweetheart's mailbox.

♥

Go on the Internet and order your sweetheart a virtual bouquet.

♥

For a whole day, call your partner by a flower name: Petunia, Daisy, Lily, Daffodil, and so on.

♥

Tickle each other with a fully bloomed rose.

♥

Ask your florist to put an arrangement in something with which your partner identifies. It could be a model pickup truck, an old running shoe, a football helmet, a favorite coffee cup—anything.

# Romantic
## proposals

What could be more ripe for romance than a marriage proposal? With four short words, one of you asks the other to share the adventures of life forever. And with a simple yes, the other person starts the dance that will lead you both to wedlock. At that instant, you and your sweetheart probably are more in love than at any other time in your relationship.

Clearly, this is a special time—and one in which what's said and how it's expressed are important. After all, the actual words of that proposal may last a moment, but the scene will live a lifetime in your memories. To inspire you and your lover, here are some stories of real-life proposals.

## He Asked Me to Marry Him in a Crowded Restaurant

"Our engagement was the most romantic day of my life, without a question. He picked me up after work on a Friday. He said we were going to downtown Chicago, to a new restaurant near the fish market. I thought, 'Oh, the aroma of fish on a hot night in Chicago.' Anyway, we drove to the warehouse district and parked in a parking garage. It was just gross. Then he took me up a stairwell onto a dark, dingy street. But when we got to the top, there was a white horse and carriage waiting for us. We

## Words of Love

Can't find quite the right way to phrase your proposal? Here are some romantic words from the past to inspire you.

"At last you are mine! Soon—in a few months, perhaps, my angel will sleep in my arms, will awaken in my arms, will live there. All your thoughts at all moments, all your looks will be for me; all my thoughts, all my moments, all my looks will be for you! My Adele!"

**—Victor Hugo to Adele Foucher**

"I hope before long to crush you in my arms and cover you with a million kisses burning as though beneath the equator."

**—Napoleon Bonaparte to Josephine**

"My heart is full of many things to say to you—Ah!—there are moments when I feel that speech is nothing after all—cheer up—remain my true, my only treasure, my all as I am yours. . . ."

**—Ludwig van Beethoven to an unidentified love**

"I never knew before, what such love as you have made me feel, was; I did not believe in it, my Fanny, was afraid of it, lest it should burn me up. But if you will love me, though there may be some fire 'twill not be more than we can bear. . . ."

**—John Keats to Fanny Brawne**

went on a ride to the fancy district. And we got dropped off outside a restaurant called the Pump Room.

"In the Pump Room there was one table that was up on a pedestal, and there were strolling violinists. We went in, and the maître d' knew exactly who I was. He escorted me to the pedestal table. There were my favorite white roses, already on the table. And once we got seated and had a drink, Kirk got on his knee. They stopped the violins. He asked me to marry him in front of 300 people. The restaurant was silent. Of course I said yes. Everyone applauded."

♥

## He Proposed on a Deserted Island

"We were at his friend's wedding on an otherwise deserted island, and my boyfriend took me out to the beach. We sat on the rocks, and he kissed me. While we were kissing, he took my hand and I felt a ring slide down my finger. We've been married for a year now."

♥

## She Proposed to Me in a Hidden Note

"We went away for a weekend together, and when I got home, I started to unpack, only to find little notes in my clothes, shoes, and toiletry bag telling me how much she cared about me and how great the weekend had been. Finally, I got to the bottom of the suitcase, and there was one final note. I opened it, and there was a proposal asking me to marry her! Darn right I said yes."

♥

## I Proposed to Her on a Mountaintop

"I took my girlfriend on a hike to a spot that we'd visited when we first started dating. When we got to the top of the trail, I asked her to marry me. It was completely unexpected. To finish off the day, I whisked her off to Baltimore's Inner Harbor for a romantic cruise on the Chesapeake. She was blown away."

♥

## I Proposed in a Sneaky Way

"My girlfriend and I had talked about marrying, and since we had both been married before, she wanted this proposal to be memorable. Well, we both work at a retail store, and I got the management to stage a scene so I could propose. The loss prevention person took my girlfriend to the back office and began telling my future bride that the reason she was called to the back was that she was guilty of employee theft. She went on to say that she knew my girlfriend had stolen something big from a fellow employee, and that the item was his heart. At that moment I walked in the door with a bouquet of roses and the ring. I got down on my knee and proposed, and through tearstained eyes she said yes."

♥

## I Saved the Best Curtain Call for Last

"A few years ago, I was starring in a community production of *Annie* with my girlfriend. We had been dating for several years, and we had talked quite seriously about marriage. I decided that the best time to ask the big question would be while the stage was mine, so I arranged to propose to my girlfriend at the end of the curtain call on closing night. When she accepted my proposal, the audience went wild. The proposal was such a success that we even had the orphans from the play in our wedding!"

# RANDOM ACTS FOR Busy Parents

# 15-Minute
## getaways

Sure, you love your kids. But parents need romance, too. The problem is, it's hard to find the time for each other when you're tending to younger kids or driving older ones all over town.

The solution? You need to find creative—and quicker—ways to celebrate your romance. If you can't get away for a weekend or even an hour, discover the pleasures of "getting away" for 15 minutes. These intimate interludes can put an unexpected spark in your day and keep the flame of your love burning bright. They'll also show you that when it comes from one harried parent to another, even the smallest gesture of love can be as heady as a night of wine and roses.

Before bed or in the morning, pop in a CD of your partner's favorite sounds of nature—the gentle roar of the ocean, the whisper of falling rain, the bird calls echoing in the forest. Snuggle up and enjoy this moment of solitude . . . together.

♥

Keep a bottle of lightly scented massage oil in your bedroom. When you both need a temporary time-out, go to your bedroom, lock the door, and give each other a short (but sweet) neck, back, and shoulder rub.

♥

Fill plastic Easter eggs with little notes detailing the reasons you love each other, or romantic memories from your past. Then take turns hiding the eggs in your yard, garden, or bedroom and hunt for each other's notes.

♥

Before the rush-rush of getting ready for school and work begins, get up a few minutes before your partner. Line the path to the bathroom with chocolate kisses. Then place a single red rose in the shower. Leave a note: "Now you know that I will kiss the ground you walk on and shower you with roses."

♥

After dinner, when the kids scatter, walk down to the local park and feed the birds together.

Send the kids outside to play or wait until they're in bed. Then, put on a CD of romantic music and take your partner in your arms for an impromptu slow dance.

♥

When it's cold outside, bundle up and walk to a nearby park to watch the sun set over a silhouette of bare trees. After the sun goes down, hurry home for huge mugs of hot cocoa.

♥

Dust off the photo album that shows you and your partner in the days before kids and mortgage payments. Page through it together while recalling your good times.

♥

Take your partner and a blanket out into the yard. Snuggle up as you watch the moon and the stars, and try to name the constellations.

♥

Get up extra early and watch the sun rise, then share a cup of coffee and a simple breakfast before the kids awaken.

♥

Invest in a bottle of fancy bubble bath, two scented candles, two extra-thick, fluffy towels, and a pint of gourmet ice cream. Take a bubble bath by candlelight . . . and spoon-feed each other your favorite flavor.

On a hot summer night before bed, invite your honey to join you under the sprinkler. There's no better way to cool off your bodies and heat up your love for one another!

♥

Bring two remote control cars to the park, sit on benches far away from each other, and chase each other around the unsuspecting pedestrians.

## Your "15-Minute Getaway" Tool Kit

When you're pressed for time, the last thing you want to do is start hunting down the ingredients for a romantic moment. Here are 10 items you can keep on hand as part of a romance "emergency kit."

♡ Massage oil
♡ Scented candles
♡ Bubble bath
♡ The thickest, softest towels and washcloths you can find
♡ A CD or two of one of the most romantic singers of all time—perhaps Frank Sinatra or Harry Connick Jr.
♡ A wicker picnic basket filled with an assortment of crackers, jars of artichoke hearts and sardines, gourmet coffee, and a small box of Godiva chocolates. Substitute fresh, crusty bread for the crackers if time permits.
♡ A bottle of good red wine
♡ A silk baby-doll nightgown (to wear or to give—flattering to every woman's figure)
♡ A bouquet of silk roses
♡ A handmade card or an original love poem written on elegant, perfumed stationery

Help wash your lover's car. And by all means, *do* start a water fight!

♥

Go out on the deck or patio and snuggle at dusk while the kids watch TV.

♥

When the skies open up, take that walk in the rain (with or without an umbrella).

♥

During the next thunderstorm, intentionally switch off the circuit breakers, killing the lights and everything else electrical (like the TV). Light dozens of candles or build a fire. Sing campfire songs or toast marshmallows with your partner and kids . . . and bask in the warmth of your love.

# Being Romantic
## despite the kids

Finding romance with your spouse may seem nearly impossible when you both are busy caring for your children. But you and your lover can find a way to keep your affections alive if you use a little imagination.

The first step to maintaining that closeness, of course, is just expressing your love. Yes, even in the midst of nursing and burping, soccer games, and music practice. Second is saving some playfulness for each other. Don't put romance on the back burner. Every little thing you do to strengthen the intimacy and unique bond you share with your spouse will spill over into your life with your children. Here are some ideas to inspire you.

Kiss your lover at least four times a day: when
you say good morning, good night, goodbye
when separating for the day, and hello when
you reunite.

♥

Display old photos from early in your
relationship. They will bring back sweet times
for the two of you, give the children a laugh,
and even encourage a memorable story or two.

♥

Likewise, tell the kids how you and your honey
met. It will help revive the special feelings you
have for each other.

♥

When you finally head to bed, undress your
partner.

## Create Your Own Special Occasions

If you seem to find time to indulge in romantic moments only on
holidays or wedding anniversaries, don't despair. Special occasions
can take on all shapes and sizes, and you can craft them around
days that are meaningful to you and your lover.

For example, one couple met on a moonlit night and now try to
take a walk together every full moon, even if the kids need to come
along. Another gives special gifts to each other on each child's
birthday, rekindling the wondrous love that led them to become a
family in the first place.

Look for events that have lifelong meaning in your relationship
and consider them an invitation to romance.

# Real-Life
## ROMANCE

"*Every night at 8 P.M., my husband and I go upstairs and read to our young daughter, who nestles between us in our bed. We never stray from that.*

*After we've read to her, we put her to bed, then return to our room for intimate time together. There's no television, no music. Sometimes we just talk about our day, our plans for the week, our frustrations, and life. But we never stray from that, either.*

*It's really the only time we connect on that level because of our busy work schedules and the time we spend caring for our daughter. There is a downside: Since all tasks and chores end at 8 P.M., our house is a wreck on most nights. But we hope our daughter will remember the reading, not the dust bunnies. And we know that the time alone closed off from the world keeps us connected, in love, and always thinking about the other.*"

♥

Stick a bottle of champagne in the snow when you get home from work. When the kids are in bed, grab your honey's hand and pull him out the door, saying you want to look at the stars. Drink a toast to your happy family.

♥

Have a little code word that you say to your partner above the chaos and the hubbub, that you both know means "I care about you and I love you."

Wear silky clothing that isn't too revealing to
be seen in around the kids but still feels and
looks alluring and soft to the touch.

♥

Hide a sexy love note or treat in the medicine
cabinet or some other place that's "off-limits"
to the children.

♥

Get rid of the TV in your bedroom.

♥

Bring home an unexpected treat for your lover
the next time you go to the store, just as you
might do for the kids.

## Romance and the Family Vacation

Getting away from day-to-day parenting duties can do wonders for your
relationship. But what do you do with the kids? Here are some ideas.

**Leave them behind.** Have the kids stay with family or friends. If you
don't usually make the childcare decisions, arranging the details for
your partner will add a special touch to your romantic plans.

**Ask for adjoining rooms.** Some hotels allow you to negotiate a lower
rate for a second room (assuming your kids are old enough to be on
their own).

**Book a suite.** All-suite hotels are ideal because parents can lavish
attention on each other while the children play or sleep in another room.

**Share the care.** Vacation with a family whose children are the same
age as yours. They can take your kids for an afternoon outing or
sleepover, and you can return the favor.

Enroll in a class together that involves
touching, such as ballroom dance. Go while the
kids are busy with another activity, or bring
them along.

## Exchanging Love Coupons

There's no better way for one harried parent to say "I love you" to
the other than to offer a little pampering. After all, when you've been
tending to a little person all day, or you're coming home to a noisy
house after a hard workday, or you just feel worn and frazzled in
general, it's nice to have someone else do your bidding for a while.

That's the idea behind exchanging love coupons that you or your
partner can redeem anytime. Not only do they provide quick relief
from a hard day, but they offer a clear expression of your love. The
unspoken message: "I love you so much that no matter what's
happening in my day, I'll set it aside to take care of you when you
need it." You can't get more romantic than that.

Here are some ideas for coupons you might give to your lover.

♡ Redeem this Love Coupon for a foot massage with your favorite
  scented oil or lotion.
♡ Redeem this Love Coupon to get me to wear the alluring outfit of
  your choice—after the kids go to bed.
♡ Redeem this Love Coupon for a long, relaxing bubble bath.
♡ Redeem this Love Coupon for an evening home alone to pamper
  yourself.
♡ Redeem this Love Coupon for a 15-minute massage right now—no
  waiting.
♡ Redeem this Love Coupon for a weekend away from washing
  dishes and cleaning up the kitchen.
♡ Redeem this Love Coupon for 1 week free from chauffeuring the
  kids to activities.
♡ Redeem this Love Coupon for a lavish day at a spa.
♡ Redeem this Love Coupon for a shower together.
♡ Redeem this Love Coupon for a new adventure—your pick!

# Extravagant
# G E S T U R E S

*One day when my husband left for work, I was exhausted and couldn't keep my eyes open. When his car was out of sight, I said heck with the housework and went to sleep in our bedroom with the air conditioner on and the phone turned off. When I awoke, the entire house was clean, fresh coffee and lunch were waiting for me on the table, beautiful flowers adorned the living room, and my husband was kneeling in the bathroom, drawing a hot bubble bath for me. Boy, I love him.*

♥

Go horseback riding as a family and spend some time riding side by side with your partner as the kids ride on ahead.

♥

Create a romantic card for your partner while the kids do their own art projects.

♥

Buy balloons for the kids at a party store, then make up a special one with a surprise tucked inside for your lover.

♥

Go out for a movie as a family, but let the kids sit up front so you can be alone together in the back. Or head to a multiplex theater where you can send the kids to their favorite flick and enjoy another one with your spouse.

Whisper something sexy in your sweetheart's ear when you're sitting down to dinner with the family.

♥

Better yet, feed the kids first and then share dinner alone with your lover.

♥

Instead of working in the yard next Saturday, spread out a blanket, lie back, and watch the clouds together.

# 12 Unique Ways
## to say "I love you"

Child rearing and romance? The two seem to go together like oil and water. After all, romance often takes a backseat to settling squabbles over the remote control or chaperoning sleepovers. The trick: Keep in mind—always—that the guy who takes out the garbage isn't just "Daddy" and the lady who makes the meals is more than "Mommy." Your partner has a name, and despite the role as parent, is still the same sweet, wonderful person you fell in love with. Here's how to bring back that lovin' feeling and share it with your sweetie when the kids aren't around—and even when they are.

Plan an all-day pajama party for two. What could be more romantic than 24 hours in your lover's arms? Hire an adult sitter or enlist a friend to take your kids for the day, then fill your bedroom with your favorite foods, romantic videos, bubble bath, and new lingerie and devote the next 24 hours to romance.

♥

Let your partner sleep in on an occasional Saturday or Sunday morning. Be sure to steal some "cuddling time" while the kids are watching cartoons.

♥

Tell him to have a light snack before he gets home. After the kids are in bed, woo him with steak, mashed potatoes, and his favorite decadent dessert.

♥

Put diamond earrings on her while she's asleep and wait for her to notice.

♥

Go to a really bad movie playing at an old-fashioned drive-in. Then engage in a good, old-fashioned make-out session.

♥

Rent him his favorite action/adventure movies—the ones you cannot stand. Then make a big batch of popcorn and watch them with him.

# Extravagant
## G E S T U R E S

*A few weeks ago during a heat wave she called me on my cell phone to see when I would be home. I was cranky and hot and told her so. When I got home, she had a nice, cool bubble bath waiting for me with candles lit. When I got into the tub, she washed my back for me. Sweet.*

♥

Send *him* flowers at the office. Roses are a classic. Send along a note: "Roses are red, violets are blue; although we have kids, I think of you too."

♥

Make a list of what you find sexiest about your partner: his long, lean legs; the way her eyes sparkle when she laughs; the way he winks at you when the kids are around. Then hide it inside a clean sock. Your partner will find it eventually!

## Alternate Ways to Say "I Love You"

Sure, "I love you" may be the most romantic phrase in the English language, but for harried parents, there are other words that are just as meaningful and just as loving.

♡ "Let's eat out."

♡ "It's my fault."

♡ "I'm so sorry."

♡ "You look beautiful."

♡ "You're a great parent."

♡ "I love the way you do that."

♡ "I am proud of you."

♡ "I'd marry you all over again."

♡ "Let's plan a weekend away."

# Real-Life ROMANCE

*She actually doesn't even know the most romantic experience I've had with her. After a long day, she fell asleep in my arms. I watched her beautifully tranquil face for 2 hours and stroked her hair. When she woke up, she rewarded me with a heartfelt kiss and told me she loved me.*

♥

In warm weather, when the windows are open, hire a musician who plays the flute or guitar to serenade your sweetheart at midnight—right under your window.

♥

Every now and then, take the kids to the video store and let them choose a movie they've been clamoring to see. While they're occupied, repair upstairs and occupy *yourselves* with each other. Snuggle, watch a video, eat junk food, and giggle like kids.

♥

When the kids are out or napping, drag out that old game of Twister. Wear something revealing, flirt outrageously, and let your lover win.

♥

When you're at the park together with the kids, throw coins in a fountain—one for each of your years together.

# RANDOM
## ACTS FOR
### *Longtime*
### *Lovers*

# Surprise Parties—
## "just because I love you"

Some people say that they hate surprises. But whether they'll admit it or not, everybody loves feeling appreciated enough to be honored with an unexpected party. For romance, a well-planned party can be just what you need to rekindle the flames and show your love. And who says you need a lot of people to throw a surprise party? The best kind is often a party for two. You can use it to celebrate a special occasion like a birthday or apply it as a spur-of-the-moment pick-me-up, or just spring something special to let your partner know you care.

Here are several ways to sneak a celebration into your partner's day.

Throw a surprise slumber party for just the two of you. Draw a bath, and when your lover's finished bathing, wrap her in a warm, fluffy towel.

♥

Book an instructor at a local dance studio and treat your partner to a few hours of instruction in romantic dances like tango, rumba, swing, and cha-cha.

♥

Host an impromptu wine-tasting party for a small group of favorite friends. Ask each couple to bring a bottle that's a tribute to their relationship—for example, Cabernet to commemorate what they drank on their wedding day or an inexpensive Zinfandel that one of them ordered on dates. Then share a sip of each wine with your lover.

♥

# Real-Life ROMANCE

*My husband isn't a big "planner," which is why I was so surprised one year when he invited more than 50 people to our house to celebrate my birthday—without my suspecting a thing. I was standing in the kitchen when all of a sudden, a huge group of cars drove up my driveway and onto the front lawn, beeping their horns. All my friends and family poured out of the cars and carried plates of food into our house to celebrate my birthday.*

# Extravagant GESTURES

"I found myself going to a local, very expensive hotel one Saturday. He opened the door to this luxurious suite, which he had apparently spent most of the previous day decorating. For the bed, he had designed a red-and-white, four-poster canopy—and in the center he had placed a red fold-out heart. Around the mirror over the vanity, he'd placed red streamers and hearts, and on the mirror, he'd written "I love you" with red lipstick. In the water pitcher were two dozen red roses, and in an ice chest two bottles of champagne were chilling. When room service delivered our dinner, I was completely swept away."

♥

Take your lover for a walk in the park and have a caterer meet you with a basket of romantic delights.

♥

Take your lover to a "hot dog and beer" party at a local ball game. Then surprise your partner by having your love announced over the public address system or displayed across the scoreboard.

♥

Do something that appeals to your lover's interests. If she's a golf nut, drive her to the course and have three of her friends meet her there for a surprise golf outing.

# Extravagant GESTURES

*" I thought that my birthday was going to be a complete bore, but my spouse made it special. She found all my past friends and hang-out buddies from high school, did research to get their phone numbers, and arranged for all of them to come to a surprise party for me. If your wife will go to those lengths for you, then that's a woman you don't let go. "*

♥

Take her on a shopping spree to pick out a new
outfit and shoes. Then tell her she'll want to
wear them for the big night on the town you
have planned.

## She Surprised Me with a Night on the Town

"On my 35th birthday, I came home from work and found a note from my wife with instructions on grooming and dress, along with an address to go to. When I arrived at the address, it turned out to be our favorite restaurant. She was there with a meal planned and drinks lined up. After a very romantic dinner, I was left in the care of the hostess, who chatted with me and kept the drinks coming. After a while the hostess answered a cell phone call from my wife, and I was off again, this time to a lingerie shop. My wife was there ready to model some things for me. I picked out a sexy outfit, and she wore it out of the store under her dress. Next, she took me to a movie. We sat in the back and kissed during the whole film. Then it was off to a hotel suite for a great night. What a birthday!"

Treat your lover to a surprise night at a karaoke bar. Sing songs that are dedicated to the special person in your life.

♥

Tuck a motel key into your sweetheart's pants pocket with directions and a note promising a night full of romance.

♥

If your sweetheart is approaching a dreaded birthday (40th, 50th, etc.), take the edge off the pain by celebrating early with a party 6 months or even a year before the date.

♥

When you give out the birthday presents, make yours a gift with several parts. Wrap them individually and make your lover guess what the next piece is. Accept a kiss as the penalty for every wrong answer.

♥

Offer your love a "scavenger hunt" meal, with each course served at the home of a different couple. Let your partner figure out where the food will be by following your clues.

# Planning
## the perfect date

What was it that first attracted you to the person you love? Was it that smile? That deep and charming personality? Or was it the great dates you went on the first few times you were together? A romantic date can help you win your lover's heart the first time. Even years later, a really good date can help you steal that person's heart all over again.

Whether you re-create your first date or do something completely out of the ordinary, an exciting, memorable date can be a great way to remind each other how strong your love truly is. Here are some suggestions to spice up your rendezvous.

Pretend to meet as strangers in a bar and get to know each other for the first time—all over again.

♥

Think of the most romantic date that the two of you have ever been on, and re-create the entire event. Go to the same restaurant, listen to the same music, and kiss good night in the same sweet way.

♥

Instead of a roaring fire, opt for something a bit more subdued. Set a tiered candelabra, complete with scented candles, anywhere you'd like to fan the flame of romance.

♥

Be a part of the town. Attend a Little League baseball game in your community and snuggle in the stands, or go to the high school play and cheer the actors.

♥

Find a sport you both enjoy (golf or tennis, for example) and spend a day in friendly competition with one another.

♥

While you're lying in bed, talk out a fantasy of a date you'd like, such as walking on a white-sand beach, feeling the cool water pass over your toes, and feeling the breeze against your skin.

# Real-Life ROMANCE

*At school, my boyfriend and I are awfully busy. Sometimes it's hard to see each other as much as we would like, so we have had to do a lot of time management and creative thinking. Since we are both graphic designers and both have to go to a copy center all the time to print out our work, we have made it our date place.*

*Sometimes we are stuck making copies for up to 6 hours. We bring cans of soda, some snacks, and a deck of cards. We sit on the floor or wherever we can find a bit of space, play card games, and have mini-picnics. Even at a place as boring as the copy center, we've learned to enjoy each other's company.*

♥

Do some volunteer work together for a local charity such as Habitat for Humanity or a soup kitchen.

♥

Re-create a great date from your past or your partner's. Whether it's your senior prom or your very first date, try to recapture the evening.

♥

On a cold winter's day, go for a sleigh ride with your sweetheart. Take hot cider, a thick blanket, and your love to keep you warm.

Have a picnic indoors. Gather 'round the plants, light candles, play your favorite romantic music, and sit on a blanket on the floor while you feed each other crackers, cheese, and strawberries.

♥

Throw a dart at a map of the area you live in. Wherever it lands, drive there for a day and find something interesting to do together.

♥

Create your own holiday traditions—a Christmas visit to illuminated gardens or a holiday pageant can become a yearly ritual.

♥

Learn something together. Go to a museum or a historic site.

## From Near-Disaster to Memorable Date

"The best date I've ever had actually happened because my car broke down on California's Highway 1 near the Big Sur coast. My girlfriend and I had been driving all day, and it was just starting to get dark. So I got a sleeping bag, some day-old potato chips, and a bottle of warm soda from the trunk. The California coast sunset was glorious that night. We found a small patch of rock-enclosed beach and had a picnic complete with candles (actually old bug torches). The date was such a success that I'm still with her today."

With take-out food and a telescope, go to the
top of a mountain and gaze at the stars—when
you're not gazing at each other.

♥

Go on a wild thrill date at an amusement park
and kiss when you're upside down on the roller
coaster.

♥

If your lover is sick, make a "sick date" out of
the ordeal. Stay at home, make chicken soup,
and watch movies together.

♥

Take your lover to the biggest toy store
you can find. Run around the store
and act like kids.

♥

# Extravagant
## G E S T U R E S

"When I was in college, I had some fraternity brothers put a table and two
chairs on an abandoned railroad bridge. I picked up my girlfriend and sug-
gested we get take-out pizza. She said that would be okay. On the way back
from picking up the pizza with her, I stopped by the railroad bridge and told
her I saw something we should check out. When we got to the bridge and
saw the table with two candles burning, she was as pleased as could be."

# Real-Life ROMANCE

"My boyfriend and I both play the guitar, so one night we just hung out at his house playing guitar together. He's been playing longer than I have, so I seldom play with him because I'm intimidated. But on that night, we just played fun, silly songs, and we really bonded. We each appreciated what the other had to offer—he taught me some cool riffs, and I sang harmonies over the melodies of his songs. Later that night, we recorded one of the songs we made up in his basement. It was wonderful just collaborating with the one I love and recognizing what marvelous talents each person can bring to something."

♥

Stage a candlelight picnic at midnight
on the lawn.

♥

After a romantic dinner, retire to the roof and
watch the stars.

♥

Simplify your lives—take a nature walk.

♥

Wait for a windy day and then go fly a kite in
an open field.

♥

Forget the movie. Go to a coffee bar where you
can reconnect.

# Celebrating
## romantic milestones

A wedding anniversary is a cherished and celebrated milestone in every married couple's life. But who says that's the only milestone you have to celebrate? There are a lot of little moments in the lives of lovers that are worth observing. Like the anniversary of your first kiss, for example. Or the date on which you proposed—something worth noting and repeating every year.

Observing unorthodox anniversaries can be a great way to revitalize your relationship. They also show that you care enough about your lover to remember all the important moments of your time together.

On the anniversary of your proposal, propose to your partner all over again. Repeat frequently.

♥

On your kids' birthdays, give your wife a card to thank her for giving you a beautiful family.

♥

On unusual holidays, rent romantic movies that are appropriate to the day and watch them together. Example: Rent *Groundhog Day* on Groundhog Day.

♥

Send roses (or her favorite flower) every month on the anniversary of the day you met.

♥

# Real-Life ROMANCE

"My husband and I secretly married on the fifth anniversary of the day we met and then held our formal wedding ceremony on another date the next year. Our reason for marrying early was hardly romantic: Money was a bit tight back then, and we hoped that being legally married might offer some tax relief to help pay for the wedding we wanted. Ten years later, we still celebrate both dates: November 15, the day we met, and May 26, our formal wedding anniversary."

# Real-Life ROMANCE

> On our 1-year anniversary of dating, I decided that I wanted to do something really special for my girlfriend. So I bought two dozen roses. I took 12 of the roses and hid them in different parts of my bedroom. With each flower was a short note telling her how special she was to me, along with directions to the next flower. When she got to the last flower, the note told her to turn around. There I was with the other 12 roses and a huge smile.

♥

Celebrate a special date for the two of you by giving a gift certificate for a star named especially for your partner.

♥

Find a calendar of unusual holidays. Pay homage to some of the weirdest ones by buying your lover an appropriate gift. Example: For the Japanese Festival of the Stars (July 7), give a crystal star.

♥

On the eve of your wedding anniversary, invite the members of your wedding party to help you re-create your bachelor and bachelorette parties (toned down as necessary, of course).

♥

Surprise her. Take her to the original place where the kiss/proposal/meeting took place, but don't tell her that it's your planned destination.

On your partner's birthday, send a thank-you
card to his or her parents—just for making
your life with your lover possible.

♥

On the anniversary of the day that you met,
take your lover to the place where you first met.
Discover each other anew.

♥

Count the number of days you have been
together and surprise your lover with a 1,000-,
5,000-, or 10,000-day anniversary
celebration.

♥

At the end of the year, on New Year's Eve, give
her a rose for every year you've been together,
with notes or poems attached to each that relate
the stages of your relationship.

♥

Commemorate the day you first bought a house
together by staying at home and beautifying
your house.

# 15 Ways
## to get your lover's attention

There comes a time in every couple's relationship when the
electricity that charged their early-marriage passion begins to
dim. He stops asking her about her dreams every morning.
She doesn't even notice when he arrives home late from
work. But the fact that the fireworks of romance aren't
exploding as frequently as they used to doesn't mean you
have to sit in the dark. With simple, caring gestures like
these, you can get your lover to look you in the eyes with that
same fire that you thought burned out years ago.

Find the same perfume or cologne you wore when you and your lover first met. Sprinkle it on generously, then greet your partner with a hug and a kiss when he gets home from work that night.

♥

Talk about the little physical things that first attracted you to one another—like those deep blue eyes or that brilliant smile.

♥

Write a romantic essay about your own "Mr. Romance" and enter it in a national competition. Read it to him even if it's not the winner.

♥

Listen for clues to the things your lover likes, then surprise him by buying one of the things he describes or doing one of the things he mentions.

♥

# Real-Life
## R O M A N C E

*One day I came home to find a trail of rose petals leading up the stairs. Every few steps, there was a candle with a note telling me to remove one item of clothing. By the time I reached the bedroom, my boyfriend was waiting for me in candlelight.*

## Real-Life ROMANCE

*While I was in the hospital after giving birth to our son, my husband gave me a certificate that he had made that said I was the most wonderful woman in the world for giving him two wonderful children and for putting up with him.*

♥

Get an elegant, new haircut.

♥

Wear his boxers or his button-down shirt
around the house.

♥

When she least expects it, look her straight in
the eyes and tell her you love her.

♥

Whisper things to him, even if you're just
telling him you're going to take out the garbage.

## He Satisfied My Sweet Tooth

"On one of our first dates I mentioned that I'd always wanted to eat a whole bowl of (only) green M&Ms and wash it down with champagne. I never said anything about it again, but 6 months later on my birthday, my boyfriend took me to a swanky hotel after a nice dinner. When I walked in the room there were 2 dozen roses, a crystal candy dish filled with green M&Ms (he'd picked them out of 20 large bags), and a bottle of Cristal champagne! What a sweetie!"

Turn the lights down low and light candles all around the house. Your eyes will glisten in the light.

♥

Listen to the music or read the writers that your sweetheart enjoys, then surprise her by starting a conversation about them.

♥

Keep "adventure" in your life—whether it's through investing, going on a whale watch, or hiking the Appalachian Trail.

♥

Be playful. Laughing together has the added advantage of lowering stress levels, and it's just plain fun!

♥

Rev up your romantic life by introducing the color pink—the color of sexual energy—into your bedroom.

♥

Think small. Big isn't always better. Try a single rose instead of a dozen, a tiny box of Godiva chocolates instead of the 5-pound variety.

♥

Use the lawn mower to carve a Cupid's heart in the lawn. Insert your name and your honey's inside.

# Making
## memories

Every minute you spend with your sweetheart is an opportunity to make a memory. It can be dramatic, like sharing the view from the top of the Statue of Liberty, or something simple, like enjoying a moonlit stroll together along a river walk.

Memories tend to just happen without much thinking—the way you probably got a crush on your lover to begin with. But you can work on making your life more memorable by having a camera on hand, saving memorabilia of times together, and keeping special times alive in your mind.

Here are some ways to ensure that you'll have lots of stories to tell your grandkids.

Each year, make a holiday decoration that symbolizes your year together—string shells from your trip to the beach, or empty glitter from your holiday party into a small glass bottle to hang.

♥

Every once in a while, spend the weekend taking pictures of everything you do together, even if it's washing dishes. Then glue the pictures to a timeline.

♥

Have a ritual for every season. Examples: Plant flowers together in the spring, build a sand castle together in the summer, bury each other in autumn leaves, and celebrate the first day of winter with a cozy fire and a shared glass of champagne.

♥

## Real-Life ROMANCE

*My husband and I got married between semesters of college, so we never really had a honeymoon. About 20 years into our marriage, we decided to finally take that special trip and went to Bermuda for 4 days. I think we appreciated it more than young couples would because we weren't exhausted from the work of planning a wedding. Afterward, I wrote him a thank-you letter, which he framed with a postcard from Bermuda. It's still hanging in our bedroom.*

# Extravagant GESTURES

*"My mom and dad got married when they were 18. My mom never had an engagement ring. So when my parents were married 20 years, my dad surprised her with a diamond ring at Christmas. But the way he gave it to her was really special. He bought her a mink coat at a consignment shop and put the ring in the pocket. It's really hard to wrap up a mink coat, so my dad wrapped a little note and sent my mom on a scavenger hunt around the house until she found the coat hanging on a wash line in our basement. She was thrilled, but she didn't find the ring until after she put the coat on and reached in the pocket. You should have seen her face!"*

♥

Create scrapbooks with pictures from trips,
tickets from movies you saw together, and
poems that remind you of each other. Look
through them together—often.

♥

Plant a tree together to commemorate
the day you met or the day you conceived
your first child.

♥

Save all the flowers that your lover gives you.
After they wilt, dry the leaves to make
your own special potpourri.

Take a ride to a place you're unfamiliar with,
and purposely get lost.

♥

Take a hometown journey. Travel to the town
your partner was born in and let your honey
relive favorite childhood memories
as you tag along.

♥

Book a murder mystery weekend with your
partner.

♥

Create a time capsule of your life and
memories together. Bury it and agree to dig it
up a few (or many) years later.

## He Turned a Study Session into a Memorable Event

"One weekend I had a ton of homework for college, but my husband wanted to get out of the house. So he forced me into the car—with me still whining about my homework. After picking up Chinese food, we drove to the Blue Ridge Parkway. He spread out a blanket and got out a picnic basket—and a copy of *Invisible Man*, the book I was supposed to be reading. After eating, we lay on the blanket, and he picked up the book and started reading to me. There we were, taking turns reading, changing our voices and expressions to fit the story. This was so sweet that I'll never forget it."

## Real-Life
### R O M A N C E

*Last year, after my 40-year-old husband and I had been married for 20 years, he sent me a dozen roses and a note saying, "Today is the day you have been in my life for half of my life. Thank you for all the wonder you've brought me."*

♥

Tell your partner how many times you've fallen in love with her throughout the years—and what triggered your feelings each time.

♥

Create your personal version of the board game Life involving all of your milestones together. Include prizes like 3-minute hugs, facial massages, get-out-of-dishwashing passes, or a night of chick flicks or karate movies.

♥

Leave an old photo of a special event from the past lying around so your lover will find it.

♥

Start an orchard or build a wall together.

♥

Jog your lover's memory. Begin conversations with the phrase, "Remember when we. . . ."

# Rediscovering
## each other

After you've been together for a while, you may begin to think you know everything about your mate. You know to get peanut M&Ms instead of the plain kind and you know to rent a horror movie instead of a drama on a Saturday night.

But the truth is, we all grow in some small way every single day. Over time, all those little changes add up. If you're not paying attention, you might miss out on your lover's new thoughts, insights, and passions.

Don't take each other for granted. Spend some time learning and growing together and use ideas like these to rekindle the fire of romance that attracted you to each other in the first place.

Write "In Search Of" personal ads and place them in the local newspaper. See if you and your lover can find each other's ad.

♥

Read old love letters to one another and talk about how your relationship has changed over the years.

♥

Play truth or dare: Tell your lover something that he has never known about you.

♥

Draw or paint pictures of each other. Don't worry if they're not masterpieces; just see what features you each think are most prominent in the other person.

♥

Try in-line skating together, and hold hands to keep each other from falling.

♥

Park your car somewhere private and steam up the windows like you used to.

♥

Record each other's New Year's resolutions, and at the end of the year, praise each other for accomplishments.

# Real-Life ROMANCE

*One night my sweetheart and I were setting the table for a dinner party when a thunderstorm made us lose electricity. We had to call our friends and cancel the party, but we ended up having a great night. Without the distractions of our guests and television, we sat down for a candlelit dinner and talked all night—something we hadn't done in a long time.*

♥

Do something together in complete silence— without feeling like you need to talk—whether it's putting together a jigsaw puzzle, visiting a museum, or working in your garden.

♥

Show a skill you haven't shown before. For example, if you're not the one who usually cooks, plan, make, and serve your mate's favorite meal—and clean up afterward.

♥

Exercise together every day for a month, taking turns choosing the type of exercise—one day, golf; the next, walking, etc.

♥

Take lessons in Vietnamese or Nuevo Latino cooking, and give a dinner party together to show off your newfound skills.

*Real-Life*
R O M A N C E

> *One night during a storm, my boyfriend and I decided to watch the rain from the porch. I don't remember what prompted us, but soon we were running around in the rain, splashing around and pushing each other into puddles as if we were 10 years old. It reminded me of what attracted me to him to begin with—his playfulness.*

♥

Reminisce about the time you first met, your
first kiss, or other important milestones, and
recall in detail how you felt.

# RANDOM ACTS
## FOR THE
## *Traveling*
## *Spouse*

# Showing
## you miss your lover

Wouldn't it be nice if you and your partner could bottle your love as a quick pick-me-up for when one of you was far away? That way, whenever the feelings of love grew faint, you could refresh it with a sip from the bottle.

That may not be possible, but there are other ways to reaffirm your love for each other while you're apart. They can be as simple as a card or flowers sent when your partner least expects it. And, of course, a thoughtful, well-chosen gift is always appropriate.

The important thing is just to show your love in some special way. Give your sweetheart something to hold on to when far away and lonely for your companionship.

Send your honey a care package with musical recordings, candies, a scented scarf, and a new picture of yourself. Add a phone card to stay in touch.

♥

Buy your partner an old-fashioned gold locket or a pocket watch with a picture of yourself inside.

♥

Put a picture of you, or both of you, in a frame on which you can record messages. Record a romantic message and hide the frame among the clothes in your lover's suitcase.

♥

Have a local radio station dedicate a song to your lover. Even if you are overseas, you can easily contact the station by e-mail, and being out of town will help you get the dedication.

♥

Send your love a ticket stub from an event you attended together in the past, along with a ticket for a future event that you will attend as soon as she returns.

♥

Buy something cute for your lover and take photos of it in all the places you visit. Present the gift and photos together with a letter about how you were thinking of your mate at each of these places.

Courting long distance? Take a picture of
yourself in each room of your home to help
your lover imagine what you are doing each day.

♥

Make a construction paper chain with a
memory that the two of you have shared on
each link. Each day you are apart, your lover
can tear off a link and enjoy the memory.

♥

Give an airline attendant a batch of your lover's
favorite cookies and ask to have them delivered
when the flight is in midair.

## Picking the Perfect Gift

If you're lucky enough to be the traveler, sending thoughtful gifts to
your loved one at home will help ease your absence. And gifts that
involve your mate's favorites are especially meaningful. For example,
if you're visiting New York and your sweetheart loves the Yankees,
you might try to get a player's autograph on a card and send it home.

Here are some other possible favorites to keep in mind when
you're picking a gift:

♡ Favorite color
♡ Favorite food
♡ Influential person your mate
   admires
♡ Favorite hobby
♡ Favorite type of music
♡ Flower your lover likes best

♡ Favorite sport/pastime
♡ Favorite fantasy
♡ Perfume/cologne your mate
   wears
♡ Favorite book
♡ Favorite cartoon character
♡ Favorite animal

# Extravagant
## G E S T U R E S

*After being married for 6 years, you would think the romance would fizzle out. On Valentine's Day a couple of years ago, I learned that that's not always true. I came home from a trip and found our house dark. As I walked in, I noticed rose petals scattered everywhere. I walked into the kitchen, and the table was set with the best dinner I've ever had. We continued the evening in the bedroom with dessert: hot fudge sundaes! Then he gave me a slow massage with hot oil. The whole night was wonderful.*

♥

Bake your spouse's favorite treat, and then send it overnight to his hotel.

♥

If you travel a lot, buy your lover a charm bracelet and add a special charm from each location you visit.

♥

If you're the one traveling, ask a friend or neighbor to deliver a dinner or presents to your partner while you are away.

♥

Away for your anniversary?
Place an advertisement proclaiming your love in the personals section of the local paper for that day.

Send flowers to your lover's hotel room, or, if
you know the location, to the office where your
mate will be working.

♥

Can't afford the real thing? Send virtual
flowers by e-mail.

♥

Right before your partner leaves, sneak love
notes into every pocket in the suitcase.

♥

Upon her return, greet your girl at the airport
dressed in a tux and carrying a rose.

♥

Buy a pair of fine men's silk pajamas. You keep
one half to wear at home while your lover wears
the other half on the trip.

♥

Instead of buying one of those books
on tape, record a book or short story
on cassette in your own voice
for your spouse to listen to on the trip.

# Keeping
## in touch

You don't have to be disconnected just because one of you is out of sight. You can say "I love you" by e-mail, instant messaging on the Web, or voice mail and pager messages. Or you can even try old-fashioned snail mail. Then there are the creative ways to stay close even without communicating. For example, in the midst of a 3-week separation, one couple planned a dinner "together." They sat down in restaurants at the same moment on opposite coasts, and they spent the meal thinking about each other.

They might have appeared to eat by themselves, but in their hearts they were not alone. And neither will you be if you try some of these ideas with your mate.

Plan to see a funny or romantic movie at the same time in your respective towns, so you can laugh or cry "together."

♥

Each of you keep a daily journal, recording what is going on in your life and describing your deepest feelings for your lover. Present it wrapped upon your return.

♥

Choose a constellation for each other. That way, when you're apart, you can look up in the sky and see your love.

♥

Create a "Reasons That I Love You" jar, and put a reason in it each day for 2 weeks before your spouse leaves. Then open the jar once your mate leaves, and send or read one reason to him each day you're apart.

♥

Wherever you and your mate may be, watch your favorite television show while eating the same snack, then call each other up afterward to share what you enjoyed about the episode.

♥

When you're away from home in a different time zone, call your spouse's work phone and leave a romantic voice mail while your mate is at home sleeping.

# Extravagant
## G E S T U R E S

> *My wife and I were separated for a while. She had to finish her internship in New York, and I'd received a job offer in Maryland. I counted up the number of days that we would be apart and bought that many Hershey's Kisses. In each one I placed a little note stating a reason that I love her. That way I was able to give her a "kiss" and tell her why I love her each and every day we had to be apart.*

♥

For shorter trips, mail a card or note a day or so in advance so it arrives at the hotel in time for your lover's stay.

♥

Cut a $100 bill in half. Each take half and upon your return, tape it together and spend it on a celebration.

♥

If you're on a long trip, start an e-mail about a future vacation you would like to take. Have your honey add to the description and send it back. Keep the story going until the two of you are together again and can actually plan the trip.

♥

Not a big writer? Send a postcard home each day with just one word from a love message. Date or number the postcards so your lover can assemble the letter.

If your mate is away for a long time, make a video of you talking about important things that have been going on in your life, so your lover can feel close to you and see your face.

♥

Get two copies of a book, fiction or nonfiction, so you both can read it while apart. Talk about it when you return.

♥

Pick up a newspaper in the area where you're staying, clip out local items you know your mate will enjoy, and mail them home.

♥

If you or your mate has a laptop computer that is connected to the Internet, go on a virtual date. Take the computer to a special place, like a museum or aquarium, then use instant messaging to chat with your mate while you're touring.

♥

## Real-Life ROMANCE

*The most romantic thing my girlfriend ever did for me was one of the simplest things. She sent me a letter while I was away on business with a poem in it that she had obviously labored over. It was at my hotel when I got there and made the time apart a little more bearable. It told me she truly cared and missed me.*

Call from a beautiful travel site and describe it
to your mate, so the two of you can enjoy it
together.

♥

Cook a dinner that you enjoy together often.
Then eat it and think of your sweetheart.

# Making
## your days apart romantic

There is no better time to fan the embers of passion than when you are apart. At the root of romance is imagination, and imagination flies free when it is untethered by routine. So nurture the romantic feelings that filled your head and heart during the early days of your love, and let them bloom again.

Put in writing the things that are in your heart but may not find their way into words when you are together. Be imaginative in ways that keep the romance alive. Most of all, make sure that in everything you do, your mate hears that special phrase, "I love you."

Buy some fine stationery and write love letters. Say all those gentle things that go unsaid but not unthought.

♥

Write your name and phone number inside a book of matches, promising a passionate time when you return. Hide the matchbook inside a pocket of a shirt your lover is taking along.

♥

Send a love letter in code, with the first letter in each line or each word spelling a message.

♥

Put dated envelopes in your lover's suitcase— one to be opened each day away—with detailed descriptions of special romantic times you've enjoyed together.

♥

Make a scented pillowcase for your lover, complete with a monogram or message. Pick a scent you can wear and your mate can sleep with, such as vanilla, and pack the pillowcase so your lover can use it while away.

♥

Send a real rose preserved within a thin coating of acrylic glaze and gold accents. Add a message that this rose will last as long as your love. Better yet, skip the acrylic and send a rose dipped in gold.

Have a very romantic photo of you made into a jigsaw puzzle. Send a piece or two with each letter.

♥

Send a mental postcard. Set a time each day when you each will spend 1 quiet minute just thinking about each other.

♥

Get two copies of a book of love poems, and each of you read the same poem each day.

♥

Send your mate a favorite shirt with a dash of your cologne on it, so that when she wears it she will think of you.

♥

# *Extravagant*
# G E S T U R E S

*I was on a business trip and having a very bad day. I had to buy another outfit for another unexpected day on the road—and I got lost trying to find the mall. Then my wallet got stolen. I came back to the hotel with a bad headache and soaked with rain. When my boyfriend called, I told him about my horrible evening, and he was very sympathetic. He suddenly said he had to go and would call back later. Fifteen minutes later, there was a knock at my door. He had called room service! They were delivering a seven-layer chocolate cake and a quart of milk to my room. I love him so much.*

Make a lipstick imprint of your lips on a card
and laminate it for his wallet.

♥

Take a lock of your hair and laminate it on the
other side of the card.

♥

Plan to go on imaginary romantic dates in your
dreams. Decide where the two of you will meet
and what you will do, then go to sleep at the
same time, thinking of meeting each other.

♥

Hide a love note where it will be found while
you're away, such as in a box of cereal.

♥

Buy a box of chocolates and under each piece
place a love note. Instruct your love to eat only
one piece a day.

# RANDOM ACTS FOR THE
## Rest of Your Life

# Working
## a little love into every day

Your love may never forget the expensive birthday present you bought or the special night the two of you watched the stars from the deck of a cruise ship. But you don't have to rely on costly gifts or exotic locations to nurture your romance. The real power of romance comes from the small acts that become part of your day-to-day life—the kind word here, the loving touch there.

All it takes is a few minutes' thought and a dash of inventiveness to develop some daily gestures that show your partner you care. Here are some suggestions that will remind both of you that you're still in love.

Fasten her necklaces and bracelets every morning.

♥

Do something that usually happens only in bed—like stroking the side of his cheek or rubbing his shoulders—at the kitchen table or while you watch TV.

♥

Tell your lover something flattering every day, whether it's about the way she smells, the curve of his biceps, her beautiful eyes—whatever.

♥

Show your mate respect in everything you do, from opening car doors to holding her chair to saying thank you when she does a favor.

♥

Hold hands in bed until you fall asleep.

♥

Provide a hug and kiss when you separate in the morning and get together again at night.

♥

Leave your lover's favorite candies lying around in places where they're sure to be found, like on top of a pillow, in a briefcase, or in a clothes drawer.

# Real-Life ROMANCE

*My boyfriend always surprises me. He makes little additions to his home, which he says remind him of me. He planted miniature roses on his balcony in my honor, has a special angel for me sitting on a shelf, and has a picture of a ballerina on his wall. Being included in his thoughts and his home in small and loving ways makes me feel touched and loved.*

♥

Give her a rose in the most sensuous way
imaginable: Tell her to close her eyes, and then
slowly, lightly brush her face with it
until the fragrance hits her nose
and the petals touch her lips.

♥

Make your lover laugh about something every
single day.

♥

Wake your lover with a kiss—every morning.

♥

Every night, remind him of something he did
that day that made you happy.

♥

Leave a loving note (with a lipstick kiss) on the
bathroom mirror or the steering wheel.

# Real-Life ROMANCE

*Through 50 years of marriage, my father kissed my mother and said "I love you" every single time he left the house. When I asked him why he did this even when he was just going to the corner store, he said, "Anytime I leave the house might be the last time I see your mother. I want 'I love you' to be my last words to her."*

♥

During the winter, warm up your lover's car in the morning.

♥

Make coffee while he's in the shower and hand him a warm cup as soon as he steps out.

♥

Greet him at the door with a kiss and a cool drink.

♥

Look at your partner's errand list and do a couple of items as a surprise.

♥

Never end a conversation without saying, "I love you."

# 12 Romantic
## ways to say "I'm sorry"

Nobody likes to say "I'm sorry," and that's probably why we all become monotone when we begin to apologize. We just want to say the words and get on with life without dwelling on our own mistakes.

But keep this in mind: Being vulnerable to a lover is the most romantic thing you can do for each other. It could also be crucial, because if your sweetheart doesn't believe that you're truly sorry, you could damage your relationship.

Anyone can utter the words, but putting some thought and time into an apology shows how much you mean it. Here are some ways you and your sweetheart can show you cherish each other.

Make an "I'll never do that again" list—with room for additions—and present it to your lover.

♥

Cook your lover a Chinese dinner with a homemade fortune cookie. When your mate cracks open the cookie, your personalized apology will be inside.

♥

Write "I'm sorry" in chalk in several places on the sidewalk along your partner's regular walking route.

♥

Hand in the towel—literally—and let your lover know you're not going to fight anymore.

♥

Videotape your apology, listing all the reasons you want your lover to forgive you, then watch it together.

♥

## *Extravagant* GESTURES

"My girlfriend worked on the second floor of a building in an office with a window. One day we had a fight. To make up, I bought a bunch of helium balloons with long strings. I wrote "I'm sorry" and "I love you" on them and let them float in front of her window."

> *After having a difficult time together and considering separation, we decided to make another go at it. My husband took all the "tough" letters that we had written to each other and burned them. Then he gave me the ashes and said, "Now those hard feelings will never come between us again."*

♥

Instead of dwelling on how sorry you are, tell your sweetheart how you're going to fix your mistake.

♥

Spell out "sorry" with rose petals on your partner's side of the bed.

♥

Send your partner a singing "I'm sorry" telegram.

♥

Record your apology on a tape, and then pop it in your sweetheart's car's cassette player so it's the first thing your love hears on the ride to work in the morning.

♥

Take her to a karaoke bar and tell her you won't stop singing until she forgives you.

# Real-Life ROMANCE

"My fiancé and I got into a big fight when we were on the phone one night. He felt so bad that he immediately hopped into the car and drove all night from Pennsylvania to my apartment in Ohio. Imagine my surprise when I opened the door early the next day to find him standing there. He handed me $200 and said that he wasn't leaving until I agreed to fly back home with him for the weekend. We hopped on the first flight back and had the most romantic weekend ever."

♥

Write your apology on the refrigerator, using magnetic poetry.

♥

Spell out "I'm sorry" in Play-Doh on your front steps so he sees it when he comes home.